Cross Stitch on Colour

Cross Stitch on Colour

Sheena Rogers

Guild of Master Craftsman Publications Ltd

First published in 1996 by
Guild of Master Craftsman Publications Ltd
166 High Street, Lewes, East Sussex BN7 1XU.

© Sheena Rogers 1996

Photos styled by Catherine Gellatly and Zul Mukhida
Photography © Zul Mukhida
All numbered drawings by John Yates,
based on sketches by Sheena Rogers
Sketches © Sheena Rogers

ISBN 0 946819 85 8

Designed by Teresa Dearlove
Typeface: Antique Olive
Printed and bound in Singapore under the supervision
of MRM Graphics, Winslow, Bucks.

To my parents

Measurements

Although care has been taken to ensure that the metric measurements are accurate, they are only conversions from imperial. In each case, by rounding up or down, the closest metric equivalent has been given. (See also the metric conversion table, page 110.)

While some materials are sold only in metric units, Imperial equivalents are given throughout for ease of use.

Materials

All of the projects featured in this book were stitched using Anchor stranded cotton threads; Madeira and DMC shade conversions are included in the keys, but exact colour matching of brands cannot be guaranteed. Please refer to the shade numbers listed.

Where the same shade is listed twice in a key, you will only need to purchase one skein of that colour, unless otherwise stated.

The fabric used throughout is Aida, 14HPI. Different materials and counts can be used, but this may alter the finished size of the work.

Blunt tapestry needles are used for each project, size 22 or 24 for cross stitch, and size 26 for quarter and three-quarter cross stitch.

Contents

Introduction

Cross stitch embroidery is the art of creating pictures by stitching small, coloured crosses onto block-weave or evenweave fabric. There are two types of cross stitch: printed cross stitch and counted cross stitch.

In printed cross stitch, the fabric already has the design printed on it, and you cover the print with your stitching. This method can give poor results as the coloured print may show through the stitches and, as the print is covered, some of the detailed features can be lost. The design might not look as accurate and the effect of your finished picture may be spoilt.

Counted cross stitch involves working from a chart onto plain fabric, by way of counting stitches and threads. It is a more accurate method and there is no chance of any pattern showing through: this is the method used throughout this book.

Most cross stitch books, charts and kits use white or cream fabrics on which to embroider the designs. Over the past few years, however, more and more craft shops and haberdasheries have been introducing new ranges of coloured cross stitch fabrics, and these can add a whole new dimension to your stitching.

The projects in this book show ideas for using these coloured fabrics in original and creative ways. Each chapter is dedicated to a different colour and for each colour, two or three contrasting projects are included.

The designs cover a wide variety of subjects, from Christmas to sport, weddings and fairgrounds. They show how a single colour background can make all the difference to the overall effect of a picture.

With each design there is a short explanation as to why subjects were stitched on certain coloured backgrounds, and how the background enhances the design.

There is also a chapter giving detailed instructions for working the various stitches required, and for following a cross stitch chart. Whatever your level of stitching experience, there are projects here for you.

Chapter 1
Materials and Skills

Cross stitch uses only a few, simple materials,
which require no great outlay, and no special work
or storage space – it is a craft open to everyone.
The basic skills, which are clearly explained in this
chapter, can be quickly learnt and with a little
practise, used to create attractive designs.

Materials
Using charts
Stitching

Materials

All you need to begin working cross stitch is fabric, threads, needles and scissors. Hoops and frames can help to keep fabric taut and stitches even, but they are not essential.

Fabrics

Fabrics can be bought either by the metre, or in small rectangles, roughly 12 x 18in (305 x 408mm). To produce evenly stitched crosses, the fabric used must be either an evenweave or a block-weave. The most widely used fabric for cross stitch is Aida. This blockweave is popular among stitchers because the small blocks formed by the woven threads, which can easily be counted, are very useful for transferring counted cross stitch designs from chart to fabric.

Hardanger and Damask resemble Aida. Small blocks are clearly visible in both of these fabrics, but Hardanger has a finer thread count than Aida and is mainly used for small, finely detailed cross stitch designs.

Damask has a shiny surface. It is often used for pillow or cushion covers and is best suited for flowery designs, because its shiny weave can

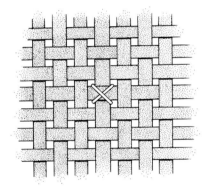

Fig 1.1 One cross stitch on Blockweave

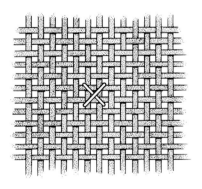

Fig 1.2 One cross stitch on Evenweave

interfere with more detailed and scenic designs.

Evenweave fabrics, such as Linda and Linen, are more difficult to cross stitch because they do not have these small blocks, but are woven with the same number of threads up and across the fabric – the warp and weft. With these, individual threads must be counted. Two or three threads on evenweave fabrics are equivalent to one small block on a blockweave fabric.

Gingham and checked fabrics may also be used for cross stitch, by embroidering one cross stitch over one square.

All evenweave and block-weave fabrics are measured by their count of holes per inch, or HPI. Common count sizes are 11, 14, 16 and 22HPI. The lower the number of holes per inch, the larger the stitches will be.

The projects in this book are all stitched on 14HPI Aida fabric, but you can use different materials and counts if you choose. If you do, remember that the finished size of your work may be altered.

Threads

The threads most commonly used for cross stitch are stranded embroidery cottons, known as Floss, though other threads can be used to create different textures. Two such threads are flower threads and perle cottons (or cotton pearl). Flower threads are very fine and produce a matt finish, whereas perle cottons have a rich, silky lustre. Stranded embroidery cottons are shinier than flower threads but not as silky as perle cottons.

Each stranded cotton is sold as either a 26½ or 33ft (8 or 10m) length which is loosely twisted upon itself to form a small bundle called a skein. Each skein is labelled with its own shade number for quick colour matching when buying new cottons. Stranded cotton threads are made up of six strands, lightly twisted together. Before stitching, these strands must be separated and then recom-bined. For the projects included in this book, you will usually combine two strands for cross stitch and use only one strand for back stitch. Gently separating each strand will also ensure that they are not twisted, and will therefore help to give an even finish to your work. It is a good idea to use lengths no longer than 16in (406mm) for stitching, to avoid knots.

Needles

For cross stitching on Aida fabrics, use either a size 22 or 24 blunt tapestry needle. For projects which involve quarter and three-quarter cross stitch, it may be easier to use a thinner and slightly sharper needle that will pierce the fabric more accurately: a size 26 needle would be ideal.

Scissors

A good pair of scissors is a must for all embroiderers, as threads need to be cleanly cut, without being pulled. For cutting fabrics, a pair of dress-makers' scissors would be useful.

Hoops and frames

Hoops and frames are optional stitching aids. They are used to hold fabric taut, helping to keep stitches even. You may find it easier to use a frame for some of the larger projects. Hand-held or floor-standing frames are made up of two 'rollers' and two side arms. The rollers each have a piece of material fixed along them, known as 'webbing'. To attach your fabric to the frame, stitch the top edge to the top roller webbing and the bottom edge to the bottom roller webbing, then unscrew one of the rollers and turn it to take up the slack. Tighten the screw and you can begin stitching, rolling the fabric up or down as you need it.

If you use a hoop, wrap the outer ring with bias binding so that your fabric does not get marked. Use a hoop which is smaller than the edges of your fabric or you may distort the material. Separate the two rings and place your fabric over the smaller of the rings. Push the larger ring over the top and tighten the ring, using the screw fixed to the edge. Always remove your fabric from the hoop at the end of each stitching session to avoid a permanent crease around your design, and never stretch your fabric too tightly, as it may become distorted.

Decorative flexi-hoops can be used both to hold your fabric while you are stitching, and to frame your picture when it is complete. Round, oval and square frames are available.

To prevent fraying, oversew all the edges of your fabric before starting any project. Fold the piece of fabric in half one way and then in half again the other to find the middle point. This is where you should start your stitching, working from the centre of your chart. It is best to centre your design before starting any project, to ensure that you will be able to fit the whole design onto the fabric.

Skills

With just a few basic cross stitch skills you can create a huge variety of patterns and designs. Almost any pattern can be worked, with colour and texture added through different combinations and uses of thread.

Starting a thread

To start stitching, pass the threaded needle through the fabric from wrong side to right, and leave about 1in (25mm) of thread on the wrong side. As you stitch, hold this loose thread against the fabric and secure it under each stitch. (See Fig 1.3.) If you prefer, you could leave the thread at the back of your work and darn it under your stitches when you have finished.

Fig 1.3 Starting a thread

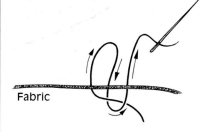

Fabric

Using charts

Counted cross stitch charts consist of small squares which are filled with either black and white symbols or colours.

Each colour cotton to be used in the design will have a different symbol or coloured square on the chart. One square on a chart represents one cross stitch.

For most projects, stitching is begun in the centre of the fabric, and from the centre of the design. As mentioned, the middle point of the fabric can be found by folding it in half lengthways, and then in half again widthways, or vice versa. Most charts have a small arrowhead at each side of the design. If lines are drawn through the arrowheads, joining top to bottom and side to side, the point at which these lines meet is the middle point of the design.

Cross stitch

A full cross stitch is shown on a chart as in Fig 1.4. To make a cross stitch, follow Fig 1.5: push the needle up at 1, down at 2, up at 3 and down again

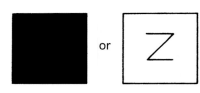

or

Fig 1.4 Symbols for full cross stitch

Fig 1.5 Full cross stitch

at 4. You have now completed one cross stitch.

Always use this method of cross stitch so that all the top stitches are in the same direction. This will give an even finish to your work.

Quarter and three-quarter cross stitch

Quarter and three-quarter cross stitch are used mainly for constructing detail and for softening edges, for example, making wheels and balls more rounded. On a chart, a quarter cross stitch is shown as in Fig 1.6. A quarter cross stitch is made by splitting one block through the middle, pushing the needle up at 1 and down at 2. (See Fig 1.7.)

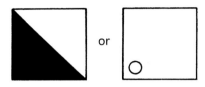

Fig 1.6 Symbols for quarter cross stitch

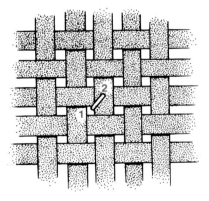

Fig 1.7 Quarter cross stitch

A three-quarter cross stitch is indicated on a chart as shown in Fig 1.8. It involves working a quarter cross stitch, followed by a half cross stitch.

For the quarter cross stitch, push the needle up at 1 and down at 2, then, for the three-quarter cross stitch, push the

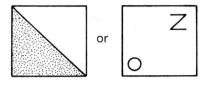

Fig 1.8 Symbols for three-quarter cross stitch

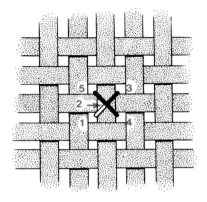

Fig 1.9 Three-quarter cross stitch

needle up at 3, down at 2, up at 4 and down at 5. (See Fig 1.9.) The first quarter would be stitched in a different colour: when two different colours or symbols occupy one square, you should stitch one quarter cross stitch in one of the colours and the other quarter and half cross stitches in the other colour.

Back stitching

Back stitch is used when all the cross stitch has been completed. It is nearly always used for outlining. On a chart, back stitch is represented by a thick line running across and around the cross stitch. To work a back stitch, follow Fig 1.10: push the needle up at 1, down at 2, up at 3, down at 1, up at 4 and back down at 3.

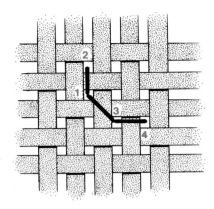

Fig 1.10 Back stitch

Finishing a thread

To finish off a piece of thread, darn about 1in (250mm) through stitches at the back of your work and carefully cut the thread close to your work. If there is a distance between areas of the same colour, it is best to finish off and start again, unless you can weave through the back of the inter-vening stitches. (See Fig 1.11.)

Pass thread through stitches at back of work . . .

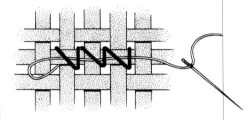

. . . and cut off close to work

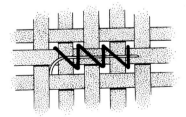

Fig 1.11 Finishing a thread

Chapter 2 Green

As well as being an effective colour on which to embroider Christmas designs, green Aida fabric has many possibilities as a grass background. Sporting designs and all kinds of animals could be stitched on this fabric; fruits, vegetables and flowers would also be suitable. Designs which would originally have been sewn onto a white background, can be seen in a different light if sewn onto green.

Strawberry
Footballer
Tennis player

Strawberry

Red and green together never fail to make a striking statement.
Here, the green Aida pushes forth the succulent fresh strawberries
and will enhance the look of a fine summer spread. This design is one that
beginners should find fairly easy to stitch, as full cross stitches are used
throughout. It is a good project to practise your cross stitch skills,
and makes an enjoyable introduction to this absorbing pastime.

Alternatives

You could also use the napkin holder design to create an attractive jam pot cover. To make a cover, cut a circle of green fabric, about 9in (229mm) in diameter and stitch the design onto the centre. To finish, trim the edge with some decorative lace.

Another idea for using the same design would be to cut 3in (760mm) strips of green fabric the same length as your kitchen shelves, and stitch a row of strawberries on each strip. Hem or fray the edges and pin to the front of your shelves.

Working the design

Napkin holder
Find the centre of your fabric and stitch the whole design, beginning where the arrows meet on the chart.

Placemat
Normally, you would start a cross stitch pattern from the centre point of both your fabric and the chart, but as this design is worked around the edge of your fabric, it is easier to begin stitching near the bottom left hand corner

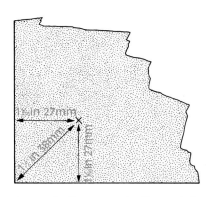

Fig 2.1 Finding your starting point

of your material, your first stitch being 1½in (38mm) from the corner (See Fig 2.1.)

Finishing

Napkin holder
When all the stitching is complete, fold one edge under ¼in (6mm), and then ¼in (6mm) again, and sew down. Repeat with the remaining three edges to form a neat hem. Join the two shorter edges together to complete your napkin holder.

Placemat
When all the cross stitch is done, you can either finish off the placemat by hemming, as for the napkin holder, or by fraying. To fray the edges you will need to machine or hand stitch a line all the way around the mat, two rows away from the last cross stitch row, and then fray each edge up to the stitched line.

Materials
Sufficient for both napkin holder and placemat

- Stranded embroidery cotton, 1 skein of each colour listed in the key
- Cotton sewing thread, green
- Aida fabric, 14HPI, green, 4 x 8in (102 x 204mm) for napkin holder; 11 x 14in (281 x 357mm) for placemat
- Finished design area: 2 x 2in (51 x 51mm) for napkin holder; 9 x 12in (228 x 305mm) for placemat

Key

	Colour	Anchor	DMC	Madeira
	White	1	Blanc	White
	Rose pink	50	605	0613
	Dark green	238	704	1308
	Light green	254	472	1414
	Scarlet red	334	606	0209
	Dark brown	359	898	2006

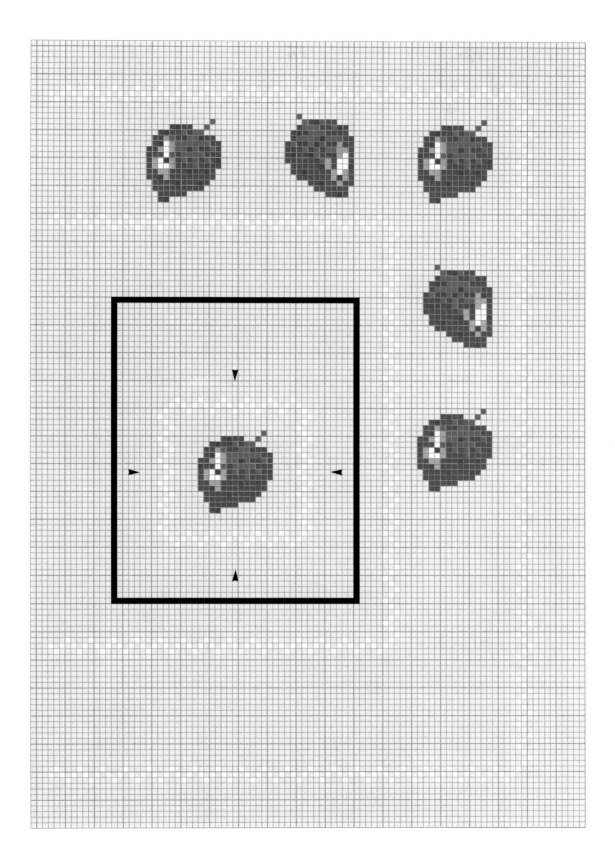

Footballer and Tennis player

The sharp green background helps to create an outdoor, sporty feel in these two designs and adds to the movement of the players. Both designs require the use of quarter and three-quarter cross stitch as well as the normal cross and back stitch, and are therefore more complex projects to work on.

Alternatives

These pictures make an ideal present for any sporting person, and could even be stitched to commemorate a match or event. Using the alphabets featured on pages 72 and 87, you could embroider the date and place of an important sporting match or event. You could also stitch the football or tennis racquet and ball on their own and mount the design in a card to send greetings to a sporting friend. Personalize the pictures by changing the eye and hair colour of the players to suit, and cross stitch a border around the edge using the appropriate team colours.

Working the design

For both the footballer and tennis player, complete all quarter, three-quarter and cross stitch, then work all the back stitch, following the black outlining on the chart.

If you prefer replace the red and orange threads of the footballer's kit with any colour variation you like. To emphasize the playing field and court, add extra stitches in appropriate colours, as shown in the completed pictures.

Materials
Sufficient for one picture

- Stranded embroidery cotton, 1 skein of each colour listed in the respective key (Certain shades of cotton may only be required for one or two stitches, e.g. blue for the eyes, and in such cases you could use leftovers from other projects that are a close match to the listed shades.)
- Aida fabric, 14HPI, green, 12 x 10in (305 x 254mm)
- Finished design area: 6¼ x 5in (159 x 127mm)

Finishing
Wash your work, if necessary, and frame it. (See Framing finished work, pages 102–104).

Key Footballer

	Colour	Anchor	DMC	Madeira
	White	1	Blanc	White
	Red	46	666	0210
	Purple	112	208	0804
	Medium sky blue	130	799	0910
	Light green	238	704	1308
	Light yellow	300	745	0111
	Dark yellow	306	783	2211
	Orange	316	740	0202
	Oak brown	358	433	2008
	Deep chocolate-brown	381	838	1914
	Light grey	398	415	1803
	Black	403	310	Black
	Pale pink	778	948	0306
	Light brown	883	3064	2312
(Back stitch)				
—	Black	403	310	Black

Key Tennis player

	Colour	Anchor	DMC	Madeira
	White	1	Blanc	White
	Red	46	666	0210
	Purple	112	208	0804
	Medium sky-blue	130	799	0910
	Pale green	259	772	1604
	Sunflower yellow	297	973	0105
	Dark yellow	306	783	2211
	Nutmeg brown	309	780	2214
	Dark brown	359	898	2006
	Light grey	398	415	1803
	Dark grey	400	317	1714
	Black	403	310	Black
	Pale pink	778	948	0306
	Light brown	883	3064	2312
(Back stitch)				
—	Black	403	310	Black

Chapter 3 Red

Red Aida, with its warm quality, has almost
always been used for sewing projects with a
Christmas theme, and this chapter would not be
complete without the inclusion of a Christmas
design. Here, however, you will also find two
projects with very different themes.

**North American
Indian-style design**

**Oriental dragon
Holly and bells**

North American Indian-style design

For a design to be successful on a red background it should incorporate many bold colours – the vivid red should not intimidate, but rather, complement the design. Although this cushion looks fairly complex to work, blocks of vivid colour form the basis of the design, and it requires only full cross stitches and a little back stitch. Experienced stitchers and beginners will find this a fun project.

Alternatives

After stitching this design, you may like to create another cushion using only the edging motif. Stitching five vertical strips an equal distance apart will make another striking design. Or try stitching long rows of the motif on a narrow piece of red Aida, and sew this strip to the edge of your curtains for a matching effect. You could also use the design to make a co-ordinating chair back or throw.

Working the design

Starting at the centre of your fabric, work the main design in cross stitch, adding the back stitch afterwards. Do not be tempted to stitch all of the black outlining first, as it is easy to misplace cross stitches this way. Next, work the patterned edging in cross stitch.

Finishing

To make up your cushion, pin the backing fabric to the Aida with right sides facing. Sew all around the cushion, 1in (25mm) from the edge, leaving an opening of about 6in (152mm), for inserting the cushion pad. To reduce fabric bulk at the corners, cut across each corner as shown in Fig 3.1.

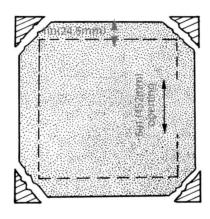

Fig 3.1 Cut the corners to reduce fabric bulk

Now turn the cushion right side out and carefully insert the cushion pad. If you are not adding piping to your cushion, sew up the whole opening using slip stitch. (See

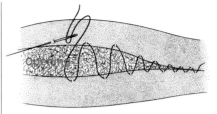

Fig 3.2 Slip stitch

Seam

Ends pushed through gap

Fig 3.3 Overlapping the edge of piping to give a neat finish

Fig 3.2.) If you do require piping, sew up the opening, leaving a 1in (25mm) gap.

To add the piping, insert one end into the gap and hold in place with a stitch. Working around the edge of the cushion, sew the piping along the seam. To finish, tuck the end into the gap, overlapping the other end, as shown in Fig 3.3, and fasten securely, ensuring that the gap is closed.

Materials

Sufficient for one cushion

- Stranded embroidery cotton, 2 skeins of black, 1 skein of all other colours listed in the key
- Cotton sewing thread, red (and black if adding piping)
- Aida fabric, 14HPI, red, 15 x 15in (381 x 381mm)
- Cotton fabric for backing, red, 15 x 15in (381 x 381mm)
- Cushion pad, 13in (330mm) square cushion
- Black piping, 5.7ft (1.75m) (optional)
- Finished design area: 10¾ x 10¾in (273 x 273mm)

Key

	Colour	Anchor	DMC	Madeira
	White	1	Blanc	White
	Light blue	161	826	1012
	Emerald green	229	701	1305
	Yellow	291	444	0106
	Bright red	335	606	0209
	Ginger brown	365	435	2010
	Black (2 skeins)	403	310	Black
	Bright blue	410	995	1102
(Back stitch)				
	Black	403	310	Black

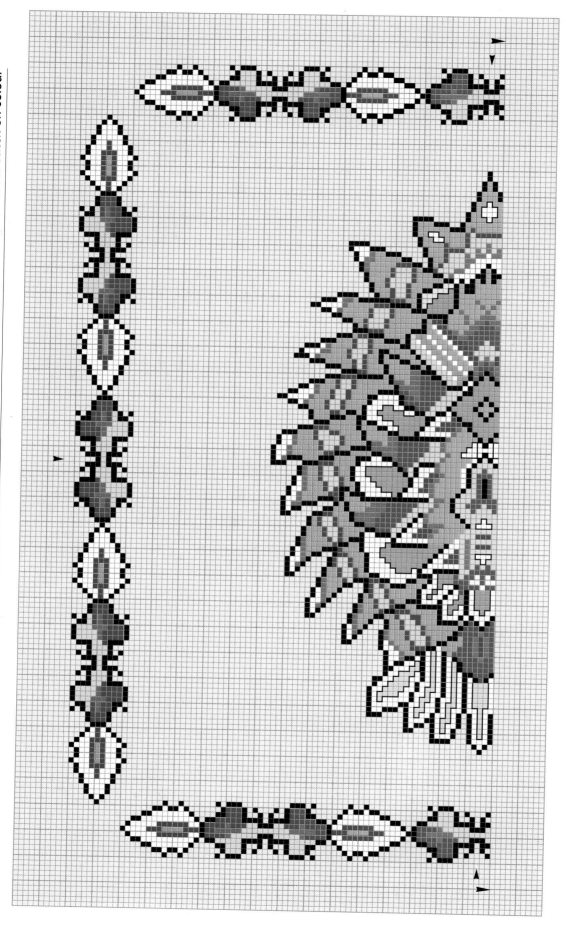

Oriental dragon

This colourful design uses the warmth of the red background
to soften the image of the dragon, and mixes light and dark shades
together to create the different textures for scales, hair and flames.
Red is associated with heat and so ties in with the dragon's flames.
The flashes of colour add to the carnival spirit.

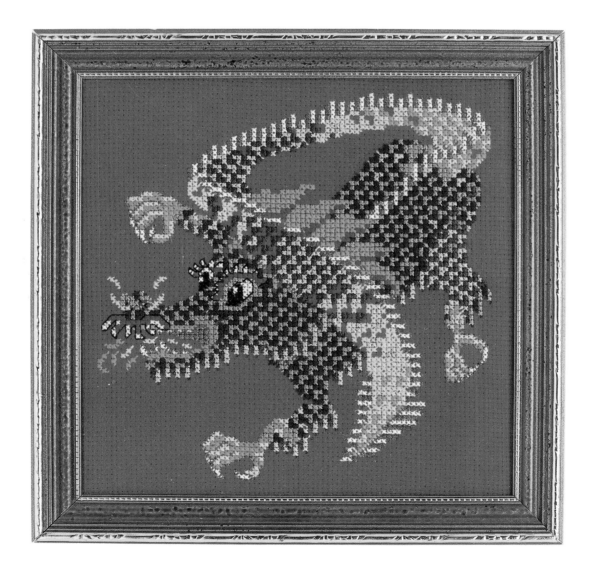

Alternatives

You could also use this dragon design to decorate a cushion cover by following the instructions given for the North American Indian-style design on page 23.

Working the design

Starting at the centre point of your fabric, complete all the cross and quarter cross stitch, using two strands of embroidery cotton.

Only a small amount of back stitch is required and this is used to outline the more detailed features. Using one strand of black cotton, back stitch around the eyes and lashes, and around the whiskers under the dragon's nose. Outline the claws and teeth as shown on the chart, using one strand of grey.

Finishing

Wash the completed work, if necessary, and frame. (See Framing finished work, pages 102–104.)

Key

	Colour	Anchor	DMC	Madeira
	White	1	Blanc	White
	Red	47	304	0509
	Pink	52	962	0609
	Dark blue	133	796	0913
	Light blue	161	826	1012
	Dark green	218	890	1314
	Light green	241	368	1310
	Yellow	297	973	0105
	Pale orange	313	977	2301
	Orange	330	608	0207
	Dark grey	400	317	1714
	Black	403	310	Black
(Back stitch)				
	Dark grey	400	317	1714
	Black	403	310	Black

Materials

Sufficient for one picture

- Stranded embroidery cotton, 1 skein of each colour listed in the key
- Aida fabric, 14HPI, red 11 x 11in (279 x 279mm)
- Finished design area: 6 x 6in (152 x 152mm)

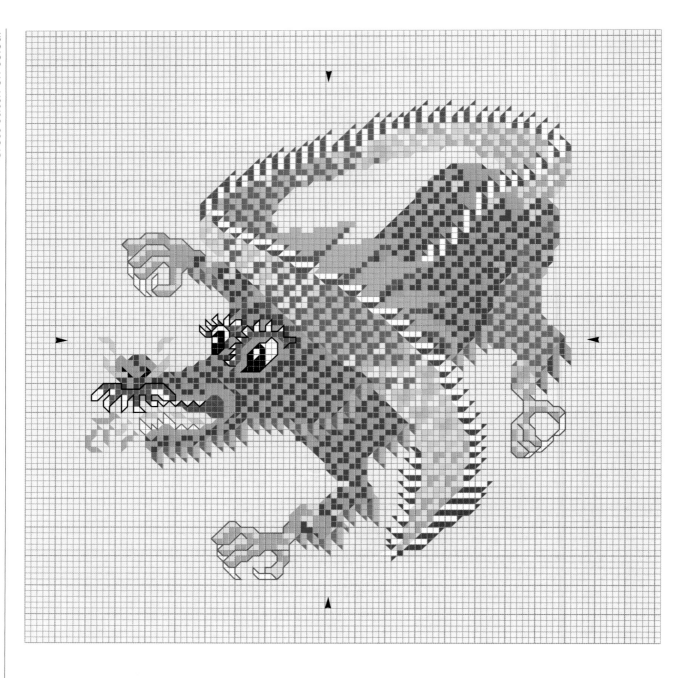

Holly and bells

The colour red is always connected with Christmas, and a flash of gold –
another Christmas colour – has also been incorporated into the card
in the shiny bells. This Christmas design is for a card and gift tag.
The card is very simple to stitch, as only full cross stitch is used.
The gift tag is slightly more detailed than the card,
as it involves some quarter cross and back stitching.

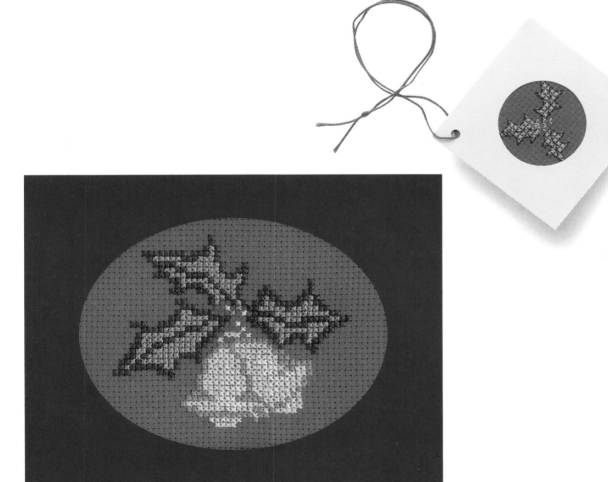

Alternatives

As well as the card and gift tag, you could use these two designs together to create a set of festive placemats for your table.

To make the placemat, refer to the strawberry placemat on page 13, but replace the green Aida with red. Stitch the zigzag pattern as shown, and then insert the holly and bells motif where the large strawberry design would be. Use the small holly design to replace the small strawberries, carefully positioning each one. Make the matching napkin holder in the same way, stitching the holly design instead of the strawberry.

The designs could also be made into Christmas tree decorations by adding a backing fabric to the stitched pieces and lightly filling them with stuffing. Attach a piece of thread to the little cushions and they are ready to hang on your tree.

Materials
Sufficient for both card and tag

- Stranded embroidery cotton, 1 skein of each colour listed in the key
- Aida fabric, 14HPI, red 4 x 5½in (102 x 140mm) for card; 2 x 2in (51 x 51mm) for tag
- **Greetings card**, blank with oval aperture, 4¼ x 6in (108 x 152mm)
- **Gift tag**, blank with circular aperture to fit
- Finished design area: 2½ x 3⅛in (64 x 79mm) for Christmas card; 1⅛ x 1⅛in (28 x 28mm) for gift tag

Working the design

Christmas card
Starting at the centre, stitch the holly and bells design using two strands of embroidery cotton.

Gift tag
First, complete the cross stitch for the red berries and the light green holly. Using one strand of white cotton, back stitch across the top and left side of each berry, and then, using one strand of dark green cotton, outline each holly leaf to complete the design.

Finishing
To make up both your card and tag, see Mounting small designs, page 104.

Key

Colour	Anchor	DMC	Madeira
White	1	Blanc	White
Red	46	666	0210
Medium green	238	704	1308
Dark green	246	986	1404
Light yellow	305	743	0113
Ginger	308	781	2213
(Back stitch)			
White	1	Blanc	White
Dark green	246	986	1404

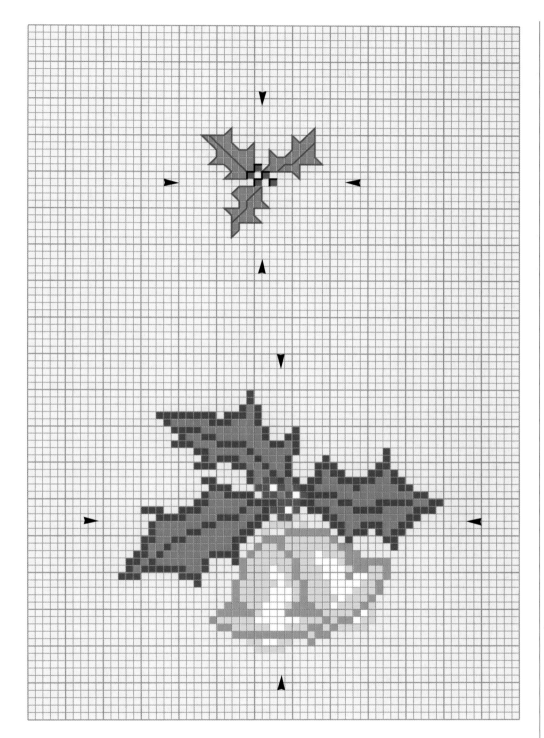

Chapter 4 Blue

Dark blue Aida covers a range of blue shades.
Some fabrics are very dark, almost black,
and some are a brighter blue.
Both hues are used for the projects in this
chapter. As a background, dark blue can
represent both the sea and the sky at night.

Tropical fish
Christmas design
Christmas fireside scene

Tropical fish

A deep blue background gives a great opportunity to show the amazing shades of colour to be found beneath the sea. Coral has been recreated using several pastel shades, with gaps in the stitching to allow flecks of the blue background to show through. Fish are stitched in electric colours and the addition of green foliage adds an element of movement to the overall effect. We may only be able to see four fish, but the blue background gives the impression that several more could be found in the distance, an effect that would be lost if the design was stitched on white. While the project uses only whole cross stitch, it does require careful thread counting.

Key

	Colour	Anchor	DMC	Madeira
	White	1	Blanc	White
	Light pink	48	963	0608
	Pink	87	3607	0708
	Dark blue	164	824	1010
	Dark green	227	702	1306
	Medium green	238	704	1308
	Light green	241	368	1310
	Sunflower yellow	297	973	0105
	Dark yellow	306	783	2211
	Orange	330	608	0207
	Tan	337	922	0310
	Pale beige	366	739	2014
	Brown	371	433	2008
	Light yellow	386	746	0101
	Black	403	310	Black
	Bright blue	410	995	1102

Alternatives

You could also use the fish pattern to make four smaller pictures, by stitching each fish individually. Greetings cards and even a hanging mobile could be made from the individual fish. The fish could also be stitched in different colours.

Materials

Sufficient for one picture

- Stranded embroidery cotton, 1 skein of each colour listed in the key
- Aida fabric, 14HPI, medium blue, 12 x 14in (305 x 356mm)
- Finished design area: 6½ x 9in (165 x 229mm)

Working the design

Starting at the centre of your fabric, complete the cross stitch, taking care when counting the threads between each part of the design. The coral on the left side of the picture is made up of many different coloured crosses, but to make it easier for stitching, you could work the edge of the coral first, and then fill in the shape with crosses placed at random.

Finishing

To mount and frame your cross stitch, see Mounting and framing, page 103–104.

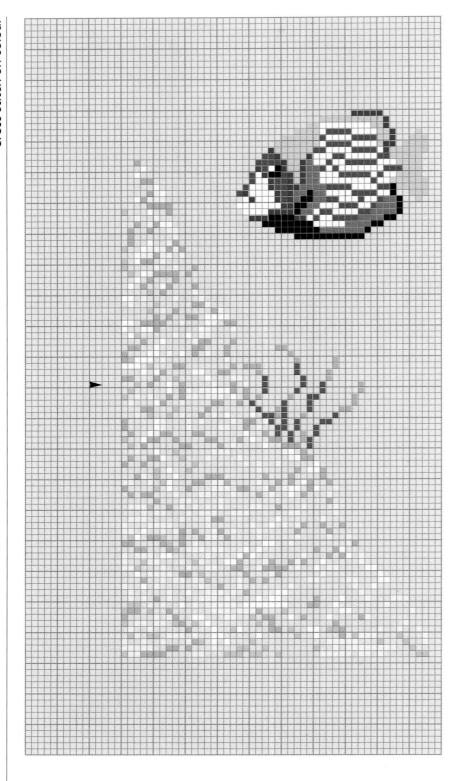

Christmas design

Dark blue is a very flexible colour to use as a background – it can represent the sea or the sky, and night-time scenes can be as tranquil or as lively as you want. In this design, houses are surrounded by the falling snow and although white is a harsh colour to stitch onto dark blue, it is toned down by the warmer brown and green hues. Yellow is also an important colour in this design because it separates the cold outdoors from the warmth inside. The effect would be very different if the windows were stitched using grey thread, as the scene would then look cold.

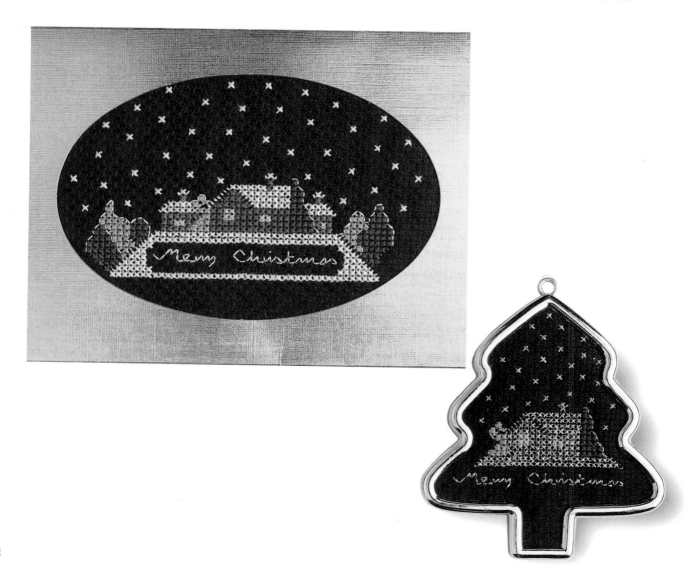

Alternatives

You may also like to use the design on a placemat, as for the strawberry design on page 13, or you could make a delightful tree ornament, using only the middle part of the picture. For an extra sparkle, try replacing the brown and white threads with gold and silver glitter threads.

The design could also be adapted to carry a larger Christmas message. Try stitching the row of houses twice, side-by-side, and finish off with the group of bushes on either side. Use the alphabets on pages 72 and 87 to create a Christmas message. Add flakes of snow and you will have a unique Christmas greeting to give or keep.

Working the design

Stitch the houses, trees and snowy hill first, following the chart. Next, you can either stitch the snow flakes as shown on the chart, or position them at random yourself. When you have done this, outline each tree and window ledge with one strand of white cotton. Finally, stitch the wording in the space under the houses.

Finishing

To mount your Christmas scene in a greetings card, see Mounting small designs, page 104.

Materials

Sufficient for one card

- Stranded embroidery cotton, 1 skein of each colour listed in the key
- Aida fabric, 14HPI, dark blue, 4 x 5½in (102 x 140mm)
- Greetings card, blank with oval aperture, 4⅛ x 6in (105 x 152mm)
- Finished design area: 2½ x 4⅛in (64 x 105mm)

Key

	Colour	Anchor	DMC	Madeira
	White	1	Blanc	White
	Light green	238	704	1308
	Dark green	246	986	1404
	Sunflower yellow	297	973	0105
	Brick brown	341	918	0314
	Dark grey	400	317	1714
(Back stitch)				
—	White	1	Blanc	White

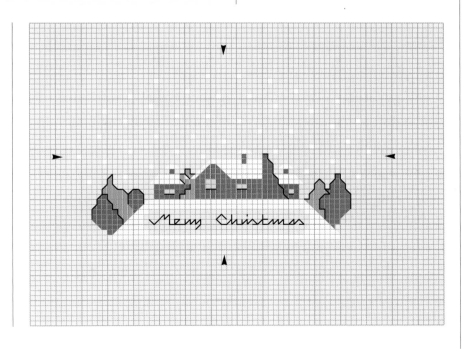

Christmas fireside scene

The warmth of this picture has been created by using rich shades of orange and brown and highlighting areas where the firelight falls in golden yellow. Again, this separates the warm interior from the dark coldness of the snowy outdoors, with the stark grey window frame parting the two extremes. This project involves many quarter cross stitches to enable more detail to be shown within the picture.

Alternatives

To give the impression of a daytime scene, you could stitch this design onto white Aida, adding some brickwork around the window.

Mount the design in a large card blank to create a Christmas card.

Working the design

Complete all the quarter cross and cross stitch first and then, using one strand of black cotton, outline each feature, using back stitch as shown on the chart.

Finishing

When all the stitching is complete, wash your fabric if necessary, and frame the picture. (See Framing finished work, pages 102–104.)

Materials
Sufficient for one picture

- Stranded embroidery cotton, 1 skein for each colour listed in the key
- Aida fabric, 14HPI, dark blue, 9 x 11in (229 x 279mm)
- Finished design area: 4x 4¾in (102 x 121mm)

Key

	Colour	Anchor	DMC	Madeira
	White	1	Blanc	White
	Pink	31	3708	0408
	Dark red	44	816	0512
	Red	47	304	0509
	Light blue	146	798	0911
	Bright green	228	911	1214
	Deep moss-green	268	937	1504
	Greengage	280	581	1609
	Golden yellow	306	783	2211
	Orange	314	741	0201
	Dark brown	360	839	1913
	Brown	365	435	2010
	Tan	369	434	2009
	Hessian	373	436	2011
	Ecru	387	Ecru	Ecru
	Light grey	398	415	1803
	Dark grey	400	317	1714
	Black	403	310	Black
	Dark blue	978	322	1004
(Back stitch)				
	Black	403	310	Black

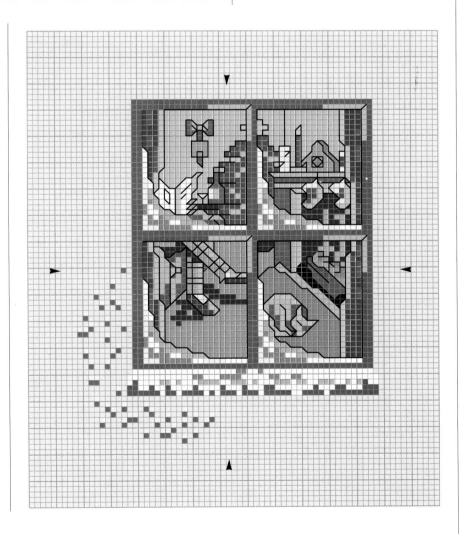

Chapter 5 Black

Black is a very versatile colour as it compliments
almost any cross stitch design and will add a
rather sophisticated touch to your work. The
designs included here have been chosen for
their contrasting qualities which helps to show
the range of possibilities that arise from using
black Aida. When working these projects it would
be a good idea to place a piece of white paper on
your lap so that the holes in the Aida can be seen
a little more clearly.

Lace-effect pattern
Floral motif
Jewelled crown

Lace-effect pattern

These two designs were created by taking the delicate, yet intricate web of lace and cross stitching it onto a solid background. The lace does not lose its delicate appearance or texture because the design consists of just one colour, giving a crisp image when stitched onto black.

44

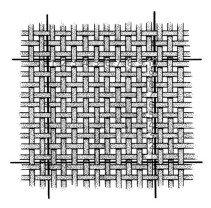

Fig 5.1 A grid of running stitch eases stitch counting

easier. Begin at the centre and work all the cross stitch before starting on the back stitch. Remove the sewing cotton when the design is complete.

Framed picture

Working from the centre of your fabric, complete all the cross stitch, using two strands of embroidery cotton, then fill in the back stitch areas, using a single strand. When the stitching is complete, frame your picture, leaving just over 1in (25mm) of black fabric all around the finished design.

Pincushion

Only one of the two pieces of Aida will be stitched, as the other piece will be used for the backing. Work the design as for the picture, using two strands of embroidery cotton for the cross stitch and one strand for the back stitch.

Alternatives

You could fill the cushion with a scented sachet to provide a delightful air freshener for any room. You may also like to reverse the white lace effect by stitching the designs onto white Aida, using black embroidery cotton, and create a co-ordinated collection of items.

Working the designs

Before starting to stitch the design, work rows of loose running stitch, 10 blocks apart, both horizontally and vertically, using sewing cotton. This will make counting, for positioning the cross stitches,

Materials
Sufficient for picture and pincushion

- Stranded embroidery cotton, 1 skein of white for each design
- Cotton sewing thread, white and black
- Aida fabric, 14HPI, black, 10 x 12½in (254 x 318mm) for picture; 2 pieces, 7½ x 7½in (191 x 191mm) for pincushion
- Filling or wadding for pincushion only
- Finished design area: 5 x 6½in (127 x 165mm) for picture; 4 x 4in (102 x 102mm) for pincushion

Key

Colour	Anchor	DMC	Madeira
(Cross stitch)			
■ White	1	Blanc	White
(Back stitch)			
— White	1	Blanc	White

Finishing

Framed picture
To frame your finished picture, follow the instructions given in Mounting and framing, pages 103–104.

Pincushion
To make up the pincushion, place the stitched piece on top of the backing, right sides out, and pin them together. Back stitch 1¼in (32mm) in from the edge, using the black thread and making sure you leave one side open for stuffing. Place the filling or wadding inside the cushion and back stitch along the remaining side. To finish, fray all the edges of the fabric up to the stitched line.

Floral motif

Black allows designs which would look pale and washed out on white
to shine through in great bursts of colour.
Here, a simple pastel bouquet of flowers appears delicate,
even though it has such a deep background,
and the use of white brings out the life in the flowers.

Alternatives

You could also use the round greetings card design to make a scented sachet, by adding 1in (250mm) to each side of the fabric, and backing the design, by stitching onto it another piece of Aida the same size, leaving a gap to insert a potpourri sachet. When this is done, sew up the gap and fray the edges.

Using one of the alphabets given in this book (see pages 72 and 87, you could also add the words 'Greetings' or 'Thank you' along the edge of the bookmark design, to make an additional card.

Materials

Sufficient for bookmark, picture and card

- Stranded embroidery cotton, 1 skein of each colour listed in the key
- Aida fabric, 14HPI, black, 2 x 6in (51 x 152mm) for bookmark; 3 x 4in (76 x 102mm) for picture; 3¼ x 3¼in (83 x 83mm) for card
- Bookmark card, blank with long, rounded aperture Greetings card, blank with circular aperture, 3¼ x 4¼in (89 x 114mm)
- Picture frame, small
- Finished design area: 1 x 4¼in (25 x 108mm) for bookmark; 1 x 2in (25 x 51mm) for picture; 2¼ x 2¼in (57 x 57mm) for greetings card

Working the design

For each item, start from the centre and complete the cross stitch bouquets, before adding the back stitch garlands to the bookmark and greetings card.

Finishing

To make up the finished items, see Mounting and framing, pages 103–104.

Key

	Colour	Anchor	DMC	Madeira
	White	1	Blanc	White
	Light pink	85	3609	0710
	Pale blue	160	813	1013
	Green	239	703	1307
	Yellow	288	445	0103
(Back stitch)				
	White	1	Blanc	White
	Green	239	703	1307

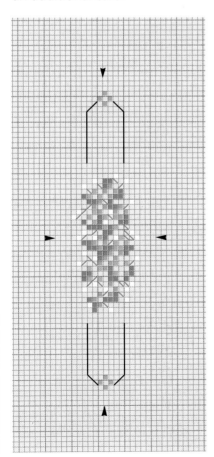

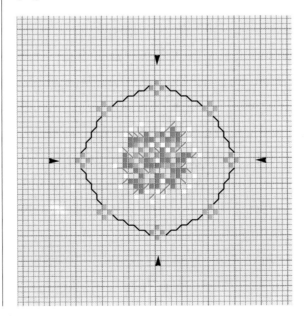

Jewelled crown

The temptation to create a design which formed a riot of colour
on a solemn black fabric could not be resisted, hence this golden crown.
The sheen of the velvet cushion was created by working with deep reds
against sorbet pinks. The coloured cottons are allowed to sing out
on the black background, but would be crushed somewhat if stitched on
white. This design is quite difficult to work as it involves a great deal
of quarter cross stitch and some very detailed back stitch.
It is therefore recommended for more experienced stitchers.

Alternatives
Instead of framing your design you could use it to make up a striking cushion (see Finishing, for North American Indian-style design, page 23) or seat cover.

You may also like to replace some of the cross stitched jewels with shiny seed beads to add sparkle.

Working the design
Because of the size of this design, the chart has been divided into two sections, spread across two pages. Find the centre of your piece of fabric and begin stitching from the centre of the chart, where lines running through the small black arrows meet.

Complete all cross and quarter cross stitch first, using two strands of cotton. Where two colours share the same square on the chart, only stitch two quarter cross stitches instead of one quarter cross stitch and one three-quarter cross stitch, as shown in Fig 5.2. This will reduce the bulkiness of thread when adding the multitude of back

Fig 5.2 Symbol for two quarter cross stitches

stitch. Add the back stitch lines with one strand of thread, using deep red for outlining the cushion, dark grey for outlining most of the white stitching and brown for the crown and tassels.

Finishing
Framing will show your work in its best light. (See Mounting and framing, pages 103–104.)

Key

Colour	Anchor	DMC	Madeira
White	1	Blanc	White
Pale pink	6	754	0305
Deep red	22	815	0513
Pink	31	3708	0408
Lipstick Red (2 skeins)	46	666	0210
Darker red	47	304	0509
Purple	102	550	0714
Dark blue	133	796	0913
Medium blue	145	334	1004
Light blue	161	826	1012
Bright green	228	911	1214
Pale green	241	368	1310
Yellow	306	783	2211
Dark gold	308	781	2213
Hessian (2 skeins)	373	436	2011
Light grey	399	414	1801
Dark grey	400	317	1714
Electric blue	410	995	1102
(Back stitch)			
Deep red	22	815	0513
Brown	341	918	0314
Dark grey	400	317	1714

Materials
Sufficient for one picture

- Stranded embroidery cotton, 2 skeins of Lipstick Red, 2 skeins of Hessian, 1 skein of all other colours listed in the key
- Aida fabric, 14HPI, black, 17 x 20in (432 x 508mm)
- Finished design area: 10¼ x 13½in (260 x 343mm)

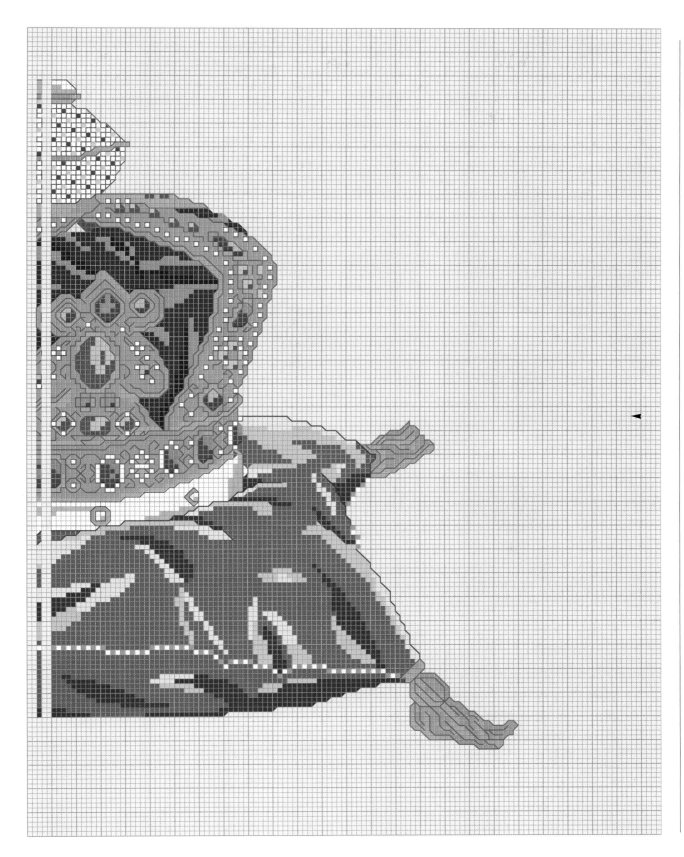

Best wishes *
of happiness in *
future,
lots of love from
Susan and Mark

Chapter 6 Pale blue

Blue Aida is a good material for enhancing the
impression of an outdoor picture, being the
colour associated with sky. Children's designs
and greetings card patterns can also be stitched
on pale blue fabric, and the coloured background
will bring a warm feel to the picture.
The designs included here all use blue fabric
to represent the sky.

Concorde
Summer fields
House

Concorde

The blue background in this design helps to push the Concorde forward,
almost bringing the picture to life, enhancing the long,
slim shape of the aircraft.

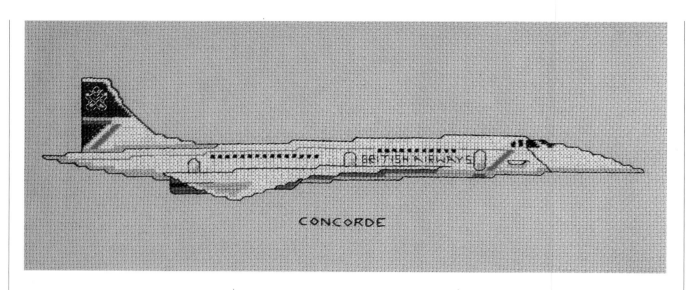

Alternatives

This design could also be used
to create an exciting chair
back, using a larger piece of
Aida fabric, or even a shelf
edging, using a narrower
piece of fabric. You could also
smarten up a towel by adding
the design about 4in (102mm)
up from its bottom edge.

Working the design

Complete all cross stitch,
starting at the centre of your
material. Using one strand of
red cotton, back stitch the line
running from the red stripe at
the front, to the tail of the
aircraft. Work the British

Materials

Sufficient for one picture

Airways logo using one strand
of blue cotton, and the
emblem on the tail fin using
one strand of white. Complete
all other back stitch using one

- Stranded embroidery cotton, 1 skein of each colour listed in
  the key
- Aida fabric, 14HPI, light blue, 9 x 16in (229 x 406mm)
- Finished design area: 3 x 11¾in (76 x 298mm)

strand of black. Count the
required number of threads
down from the bottom of the
aircraft, and back stitch the
word `Concorde', using black
cotton.

Finishing

To frame your completed
Concorde, follow the instructions given in Mounting and
framing, pages 103–104.

Key

	Colour	Anchor	DMC	Madeira
	White	1	Blanc	White
	Red	46	666	0210
	Blue	133	796	0913
	Light grey	398	415	1803
	Dark grey	400	317	1714
	Black	403	310	Black
(Back stitch)				
	White (for tail emblem)	1	Blanc	White
	Black (for outlining)	403	310	Black
	Red	46	666	0210
	Blue	133	796	0913

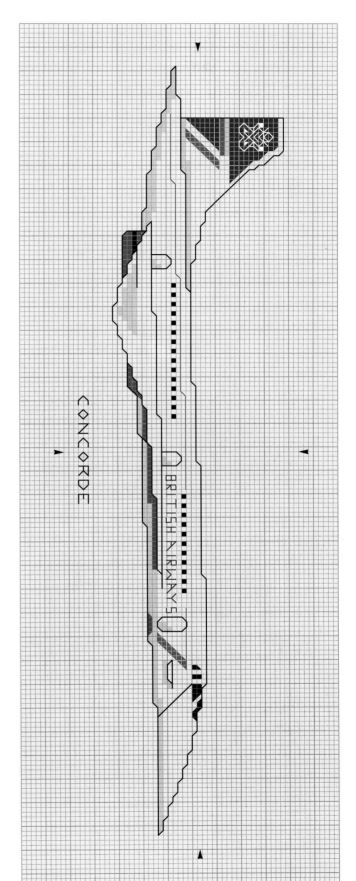

CONCORDE

BRITISH AIRWAYS

Summer fields

While most of the background is covered in this project,
the pale blue serves its purpose by softening the edges of the fields and
toning down the many bright colours used to create this countryside scene.
It also creates a harmonious effect between land and sky.
Too many deep colours together would look out of place against the pale sky,
so some specks of blue Aida have been allowed to show through.

Alternatives

The blue background of this project helped to provide the feeling of a summer's day, but you could stitch this same design onto a pale brown background for an autumn picture. Add white stitches to the tops of the hedges and you will have a wintery scene.

Working the design

Complete all the cross stitch as shown on the chart and then the quarter cross stitch on the more detailed features, such as the sheep, hay bales and roof tops. With one strand of dark brown cotton, back stitch the six hay bales and the fences. Using one strand of white cotton, back stitch the gulls following the tractor. With one strand of black cotton, complete the remaining back stitch, including the remaining gulls. Referring to the chart, work two lines of back stitch around the finished design.

Finishing

Follow the instructions for framing your cross stitch, given in Mounting and framing, pages 103–104.

Materials

Sufficient for one picture

- Stranded embroidery cottons, 1 skein of each colour listed in the key (As there are many different colours listed, you could substitute some shades with threads you already have, maybe leftovers from other projects. You may also like to experiment with different shades to obtain even more varied fields.)
- Aida fabric, 14 HPI, light blue, 11 x 13in (279 x 330mm)
- Finished design area: 5½ x 8in (140 x 203mm)

Key

	Colour	Anchor	DMC	Madeira
	White	1	Blanc	White
	Red	46	666	0210
	Forget-me-not blue	146	798	0911
	Light turquoise	185	964	1112
	Light leaf-green	226	702	1306
	Light green	241	368	1310
	Medium deep-green	245	700	1304
	Dark green	246	986	1404
	Lettuce green	254	472	1414
	Parrot green	256	906	1411
	Pale green	259	772	1604
	Deep moss-green	268	937	1504
	Greengage	280	581	1609
	Lemon yellow	289	307	0104
	Dark yellow	306	783	2211
	Ginger	308	781	2213
	Dark brown	360	839	1913
	Ginger brown	365	435	2010
	Pale beige	366	739	2014
	Brown	371	433	2008
	Light grey	399	414	1801
	Dark grey	400	317	1714
	Black	403	310	Black
	Green-brown	832	612	1910
(Back stitch)				
	White (for seagulls)	1	Blanc	White
	Dark brown (for fences)	360	839	1913
	Black (for outlining)	403	310	Black

House

In this scene the pale blue gives a summer feel and softens all the edges
in the design. The clusters of flowers in front of the house
are in bloom and everything looks peaceful.

Alternatives

Although this design makes a colourful 'Welcome to your new home' card or birthday card, you could also frame the design for a dainty picture.

You could also create a scented sachet, sandwiching some pot pourri between the Aida and a piece of backing fabric, or fray the edges of the design to make a small coaster.

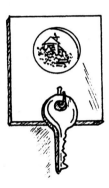

Working the design

Work the whole design in full cross stitch. Using one strand of dark brown cotton, back stitch five lines to indicate the steps. Outline the house and beams using one strand of black. Carefully work the black leaded windows in back stitch to complete the design.

To obtain a more even surface to the picture, you could work the windows in a slightly different way. Before working the back stitch, work

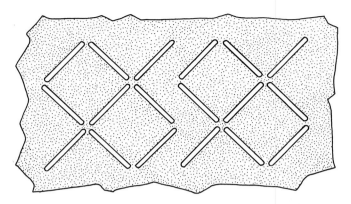

Fig 6.1 For a more even window surface, first work half cross stitch with two white strands . . .

. . . then cross each white stitch with one black strand

half cross stitch using two strands of white cotton, placing each stitch in the directions shown, then, with one strand of black cotton, cross each white stitch by working half cross stitch on top of the white thread, in the directions shown. When you have done this, work the outline around the edge and through the middle of the window, using back stitch.

This method can also be used in other projects, where outlining in backstitch and the main threads of cross stitch occupy one square on the chart, to help reduce thread bulk.

Finishing

Cut the Aida to fit inside the card and follow the instructions given in Mounting small designs, page 104.

Materials
Sufficient for one picture

- Stranded embroidery cotton, 1 skein of each colour listed in the key
- Aida fabric, 14HPI, pale blue, 4 x 4in (102 x 102mm)
- Greetings card, blank with circular aperture to fit
- Finished design area: 2 x 2¼in (51 x 57mm)

Key

	Colour	Anchor	DMC	Madeira
	White	1	Blanc	White
	Red	46	666	0210
	Deep pink	52	962	0609
	Dark green	229	700	1304
	Light green	254	472	1414
	Sunflower yellow	297	973	0105
	Deep brown	359	898	2006
	Light grey	398	415	1803
	Electric blue	410	995	1102
	Light brown	883	3064	2312
(Back stitch)				
—	Black	403	310	Black
—	Deep brown	359	898	2006

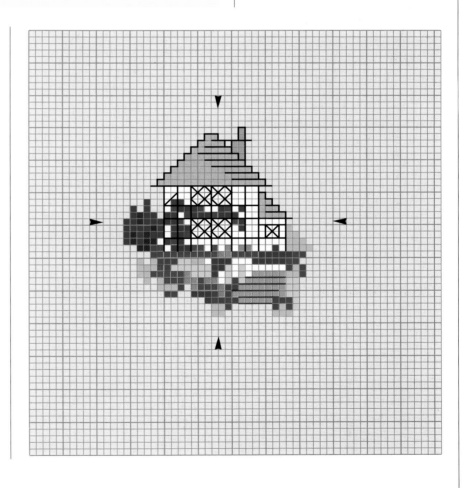

Chapter 7 Pale pink

The scope for successful designs on pale pink
fabric is fairly limited, as the colour cannot be
used to represent land, sea or sky.
It is best to use this colour background purely
for decorative or commemorative designs,
examples of which are featured in this chapter.

Birth sampler
Carousel
Rosebud

Birth sampler

Both pale pink and pale blue fabrics can be successfully used
in children's designs, and this design was created so that it could
be stitched on either. It was more difficult to produce a design of animals
on pale pink than blue as the blue ties in naturally with the sky,
but the pink adds a fairytale quality to the work.

Alternatives

You could also use the baby
and cot design on its own to
make a special card, and
personalize it using the given
alphabets. The lettering can be
used to personalize any of the
projects in this book.

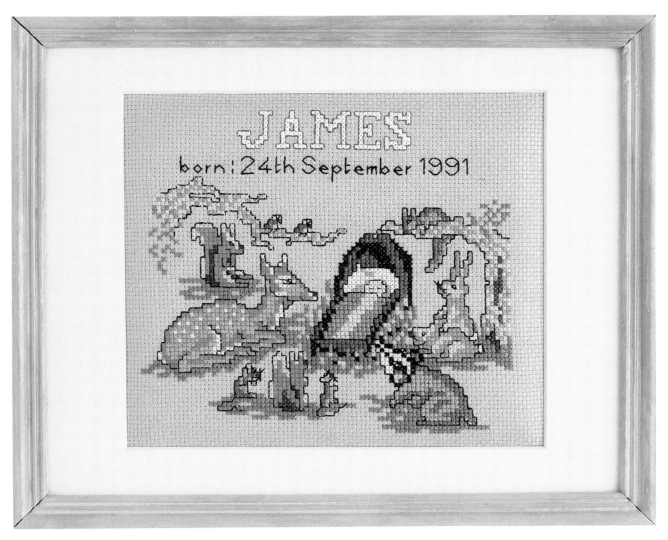

Working the design

The pattern used for both the boy's and the girl's sampler is the same, the only difference being the colours of the baby's blankets and the outline of the name.

Beginning at the centre of your fabric, cross stitch the design, using the appropriate threads for the child's bedding. Complete all back stitch outlining as shown on the chart. Using the small alphabet provided, draw out the date of birth, leaving a gap of one square between each letter and two squares between each word. Centre the wording and date around the vertical centre line, and back stitch using one strand of black cotton. Using the larger alphabet, draw out the name of the child, again leaving a gap of one square between each letter. Centre the name at the point marked on the chart and cross stitch the design using two strands of white cotton. With one strand of pink thread for the girl sampler, or blue thread for the boy, outline the lettering in back stitch. Your sampler is now complete.

Finishing

Framing your sampler will protect and enhance it. (See Mounting and framing, pages 103–104.)

Materials

Sufficient for one sampler

- Stranded embroidery cotton, 1 skein of each colour listed in the key
- Aida fabric, 14HPI, pale pink or pale blue, 10 x 12in (254 x 305mm)
- Finished design area: 5½ x 6¼in (140 x 158mm)

Key

Colour	Anchor	DMC	Madeira
White	1	Blanc	White
Pink	50	605	0613
Dark blue	127	791	0904
Green	239	703	1307
Yellow	305	743	0113
Gold	308	781	2213
Peach	337	922	0310
Red brown	339	920	0312
Dark cream	366	739	2014
Light brown	378	841	1911
Dark brown	381	838	1914
Light grey	399	414	1801
Dark grey	400	317	1714
Black	403	310	Black
Palest pink	778	948	0306
Medium blue	978	322	1004
Pale pink (for girl)	48	963	0608
Pale blue (for boy)	159	827	1014
Dark pink (for girl)	54	956	0611
Blue (for boy)	161	826	1012
(Back stitch)			
Dark pink (for girl)	54	956	0611
Blue (for boy)	161	826	1012
Black	403	310	Black

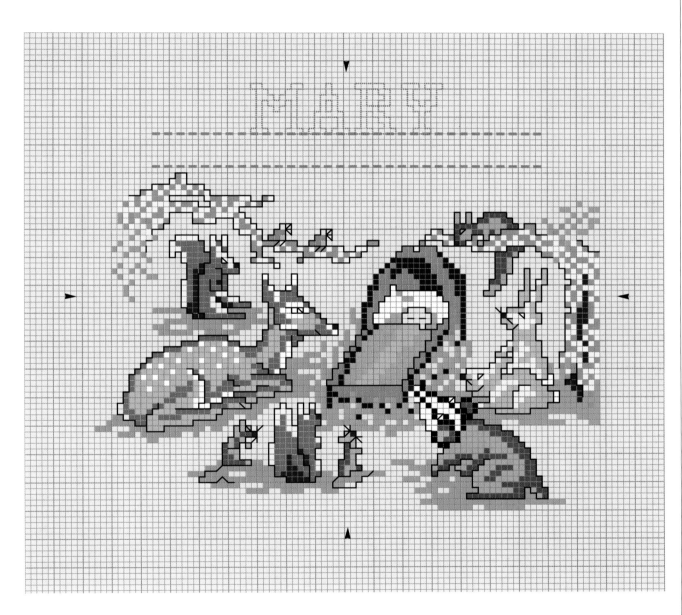

Carousel

Sweet pastel colours are associated with children and any
toy designs can be successfully stitched on them. The fairytale carousel here
uses all the pastel shades to create a soft, dreamy effect and the pale pink
background enhances the shades of the design. Three horses are visible and,
to be correct, there should be a fourth at the back of the carousel, but to
keep the design fairly simple, this horse has been omitted.

Alternatives

The decorative patterns featured on the top and bottom of the carousel could be added to other designs to make attractive borders.

You could also use parts of the design to make a wonderful hanging mobile for a child's room. Stitch the top triangle of the carousel and cut the fabric to 1in (25mm) around the

Materials

Sufficient for one picture

- Stranded embroidery cotton, 1 skein of each colour listed in the key
- Aida fabric, 14HPI, pale pink, 12 x 14in (305 x 356mm)
- Finished design area: 6½ x 8in (165 x 203mm)

edges. Repeat this part of the design on a second piece of Aida and, again, cut around the edge, 1in (25mm) from the design. With right sides facing, sew the two pieces together, about two rows from the design, rounding all the edges and leaving a 3in (76mm) gap at the bottom. Cut a few careful snips into the fabric at the corners to reduce fabric bulk when turning right sides out, then lightly fill with toy stuffing. Sew up the gap.

Follow the main horse design on the chart, changing the mane colours if you wish, and stitch three horses. As with the top of the carousel, back the horses, but use pink fabric (preferably felt) and stuff lightly. Attach pieces of thread to the saddles of the horses and the other ends to the bottom edge of the carousel top, varying the

length so that the horses hang at different heights. Fix a thread to the very top of the carousel and your mobile is ready to hang.

Working the design

Complete all quarter, three-quarter and cross stitch, following the chart. With one strand of black cotton, back stitch all of the outlining.

Finishing

To frame your carousel, follow the instructions given in Mounting and framing, pages 103–104.

Key

	Colour	Anchor	DMC	Madeira
	White	1	Blanc	White
	Pink	55	957	0612
	Blue	161	826	1012
	Green	238	704	1308
	Pale green	254	472	1414
	Yellow	298	972	0107
	Pale yellow	301	744	0112
	Ginger brown	308	781	2213
	Beige	366	739	2014
	Light grey	398	415	1803
	Black	403	310	Black
(Back stitch)				
—	Black	403	310	Black

Rosebud

Pink is a challenging colour on which to embroider flowers.
Most flowers are made up of so many different shades that the pink
background can easily dominate. This tight rosebud design
consists of deep shades, and the pink background
adds to its delicate, young appearance.

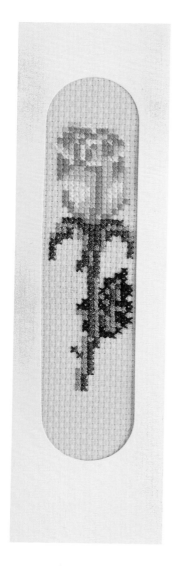

Alternatives

You could also use this design to make a stylish curtain edging. Use two long strips of Aida fabric to fit the curtains (measuring from the top edge of each curtain to the bottom edge), and repeat the rosebud design down each strip, leaving a reasonable space between each repeat. Fold the edges of the fabric under and stitch the strips to the front of the curtains, along the inside edges.

You could even stitch more rosebud strips to make a striped set of curtains. Stitch the rosebud petals using shades of blue, yellow, pink or any other colour that would co-ordinate with your decor.

Working the design

Following the chart, work the cross stitch design. If you wish to do so, back stitch an outline around the design to define the leaves and petals in more detail, using one strand of deep red-mauve thread.

Finishing

Mount your finished work in the card blank. (See Mounting small designs, page 104.)

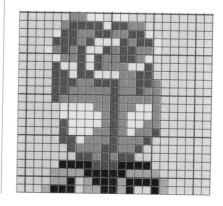

Materials

Sufficient for one bookmark

- Stranded embroidery cotton, 1 skein of each colour listed in the key
- Aida fabric, 14HPI, pale pink, 2 x 6½in (51 x 165mm)
- Bookmark card, blank, white, aperture size 1¼ x 5in (32 x 127mm)
- Finished design area: 1⅛ x 3½in (28 x 89mm)

Key

Colour	Anchor	DMC	Madeira
Light pink	48	963	0608
Deep red/mauve	72	902	0601
Lilac pink	85	3609	0710
Dark pink	87	3607	0708
Dark green	246	986	1404
Light green	280	581	1609

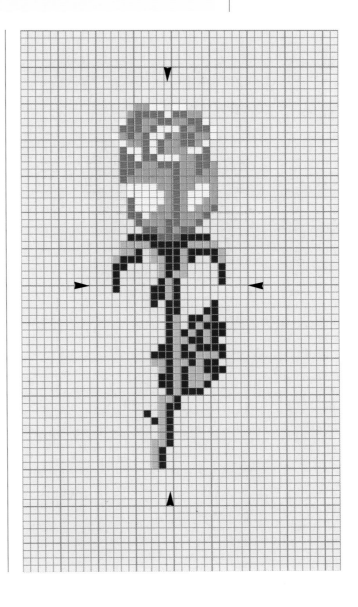

Chapter 8 Pale brown

Many shades of pale brown Aida can be found at good craft stores, ranging from a light, creamy brown to a darker, earthy colour.
For stitching projects, pale brown makes a good base on which to embroider birds and animals, plant life, buildings and even designs for special occasions or events.

Sphinx and pyramids
Goldfinches
Wedding design

sphinx and pyramids

The earthy quality of the pale brown Aida is what makes this design realistic. Shades of yellow and brown create the objects that are scattered across the sand, and the background helps to bring these objects and the sand together, so that they appear to be made of the same material. The few wisps of blue thread separate the sand from the sky, but the pale brown of the sky does not look out of place as the eye is forced to look into the hazy distance.

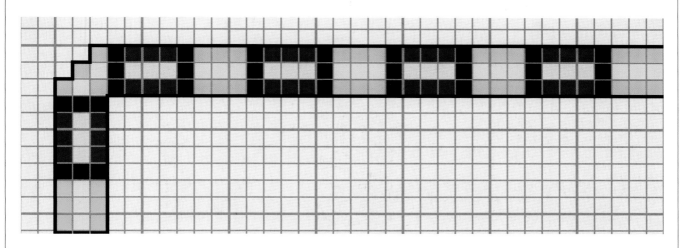

Alternatives

To make a zip purse for postcards or notes, take another piece of fabric the same size as the picture, place this and the design right sides together, and stitch around the bottom and sides, leaving the top edge open for the zip. Stitch the zip in place, turn the purse right side out, and you have a unique accessory.

Materials

Sufficient for one picture

- Stranded embroidery cotton, 1 skein of each colour listed in the key
- Aida fabric, 14HPI, pale brown, 8 x 10in (203 x 254mm)
- Finished design area: 4 x 5½in (102 x 140mm)

Use the border pattern alone for a striking geometric design

Working the design

Beginning at the centre point, complete all the cross stitch. Using one strand of brown thread, back stitch the outlining of the sphinx. Outline the blue and gold edging with one strand of black cotton.

Finishing

To add a richer feel to the whole picture, try framing the design in a marbled frame or a frame with a gold edge. (See Mounting and framing, pages 103–104.)

Key

	Colour	Anchor	DMC	Madeira
	Pale sky-blue	128	800	0908
	Deep saphire-blue	133	796	0913
	Light yellow	301	744	0112
	Dark yellow	306	783	2211
	Ginger	308	781	2213
	Oak brown	358	433	2008
	Hessian	373	436	2011
	Coffee	378	841	1911
	Light grey	398	415	1803
	Black	403	310	Black
(Back stitch)				
—	Oak brown	358	433	2008
—	Black	403	310	Black

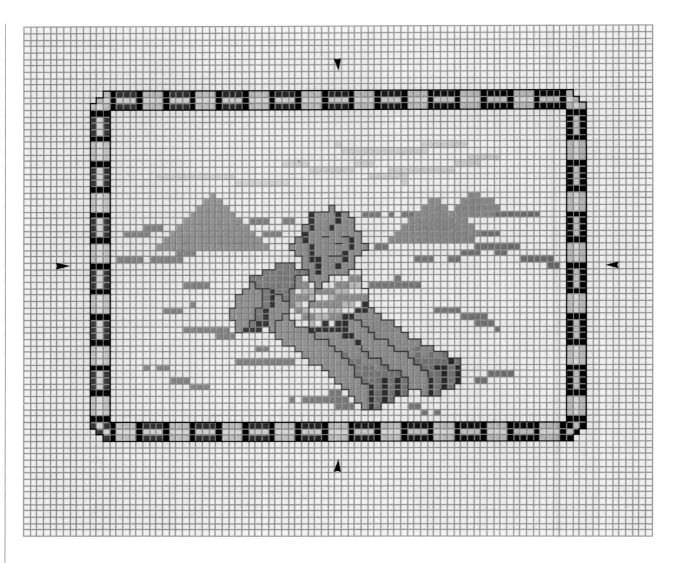

Goldfinches

Here, the brown fabric represents a woody tree, and subdued colours
were chosen to mingle in with the surroundings and look natural.
The adult goldfinch, however, was stitched with deeper shades
to show the beauty of its patterns. The leaf border was added
to give the impression of peering through the leaves
so as not to disturb the young family of birds.

Alternatives

If you do not want to frame your design, you could fray the four edges close to the stitching and use it as a decorative placemat or coaster.

You could also use the leaf edging motif to add a border to a Christmas design. Stitch the edging as a continuous round and place one of the small Christmas designs featured in this book in the centre. Use deeper green shades of thread and add a few red cross stitches here and there to create the look of Holly.

Working the design

First, cross stitch the birds, nest and branch. Work the leaves in the two opposite corners. With one strand of dark grey thread, outline the branch in back stitch. Back stitch around the nest using 1 strand of green-brown cotton as shown on the chart, and back stitch using one strand of black to define the birds eyes and beaks, and the

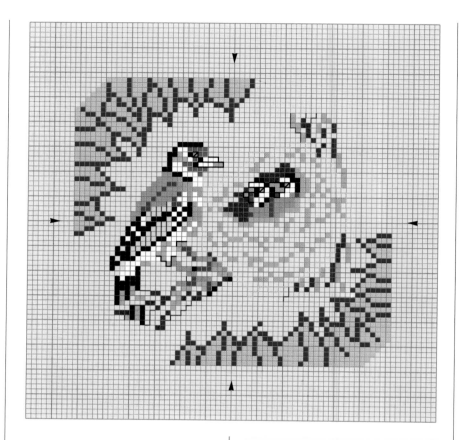

remaining detail on the large goldfinch.

Finishing

A square, woodgrain flexi-hoop, 4 x 4in (102 x 102mm), can be used as a frame, and will enhance your finished picture. (See Flexi-hoops, page 105.)

Key

	Colour	Anchor	DMC	Madeira
	White	1	Blanc	White
	Red	46	666	0210
	Light green	241	368	1310
	Yellow	305	743	0113
	Oak brown	358	433	2008
	Hessian	373	436	2011
	Coffee	378	841	1911
	Light grey	398	415	1803
	Dark grey	400	317	1714
	Black	403	310	Black
	Green-brown	832	612	1910
	Dark green	923	699	1303
(Back stitch)				
—	Dark grey	400	317	1714
—	Black	403	310	Black
—	Green-brown	832	612	1910

Materials

Sufficient for one picture

- Stranded embroidery cotton, 1 skein of each colour listed in the key
- Aida fabric, 14HPI, pale brown, 9 x 9in (229 x 229mm)
- Finished design area: 4 x 4in (102 x 102mm)

Wedding design

Pale brown fabric allows the traditional white of weddings to be used
in lots of decorative motifs, and this has been used to advantage
by including white columns wrapped in glorious flowers.
Using small motifs in the design also enables you
to make matching accessories.

Motifs could also be used to make a cake band – form a strip of the motifs to wrap around the cake.

Working the design

For both the card and the sampler, use only one strand of thread for all stitching, as using two strands will give a harsh appearance to the finished picture.

Card

On a piece of graph paper or hand-drawn square grid, chart the names of the bride and groom, referring to the photo-graph and the chart and using the alphabet provided. Do the same for the date of the wedding, leaving a gap of two squares between the month and the date. Count the number of squares each word covers to find the centre of each word. When stitching the design, line up each word on the centre points shown on the chart. Using one strand at a time, complete the cross stitch design and the back stitch wording.

Alternatives

The small 'bow and bells' motif could also be used to create an anniversary card, using the alphabets provided to add the wording. The 'hearts and flowers' motif could be used in the same way, creating a delightful birthday greeting, or even a thank you card.

Key

Colour		Anchor	DMC	Madeira
	White	1	Blanc	White
	Light pink	31	3708	0408
	Dark pink	35	3705	0410
	Blue	161	826	1012
	Dark green	228	911	1214
	Light green	238	704	1308
	Brown	358	433	2008
	Cream-beige	373	436	2011
	Light grey	398	415	1803
	Dark grey	400	317	1714
	Black	403	310	Black
	Palest pink	778	948	0306
(Back stitch)				
	Blue	161	826	1012
	Dark green	228	911	1214
	Light green	238	704	1308
	Dark grey	400	317	1714
	Black	403	310	Black

Materials
Sufficient for wedding card and sampler

- Stranded embroidery cotton, 1 skein of each colour listed in the key
- Aida fabric, 14HPI, pale brown, 4½ x 6in (114 x 152mm) for card; 11 x 11in (279 x 279mm) for sampler
- Greetings card, blank with church window or rectangular aperture, size of aperture 3 x 4½in (76 x 114mm)
- Finished design area: 2¼ x 4in (57 x 102mm) for the card; 6 x 6in (152 x 152mm) for the sampler

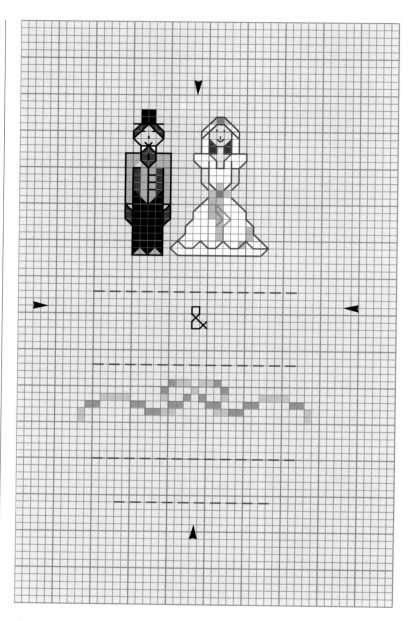

Sampler

Chart the names of the bride and groom as for the card, but this time put both names on the one line, with an ampersand in between them. Leave a space of two squares between each word. (See Fig 8.13 and photo of completed project.) Centre the wording at the point marked on the chart. Do the same with the date, again leaving two squares between each word. Centre this wording as marked. Chart the name of the church, but this time leave only one square between each word. If the title is very long, split the wording into two lines, centreing both.

You can now begin stitching the design, by following the chart and the directions for the card.

Finishing

Card

Mount the finished design in the card blank, following the instructions given in Mounting small designs, page 106.

Sampler

Frame your finished sampler as you choose. (See Mounting and framing, pages 103–104.)

Chapter 9 Pale green

Pale green is a very cold colour on which to work your projects. This means that the design needs to be fairly bold, using sharp, deep shades of thread so that the picture does not look drained of colour. As a background, light green can be used to represent ice or water. Stitching polar bears, skiers or wintery scenes onto light green fabrics will create very pleasing effects.

Figure skater
Frog and water lily
Flowers on trellis

Figure skater

This project uses the cold quality of pale green Aida to represent ice, and the back stitched tracks of the skater help to give the impression of motion. The dark shades of the skater's gloves and hair help push the figure into the foreground, and her skin looks radiant against the pale background.

Alternatives

This design could also be added to a winter scarf by stitching the whole panel to one end of the scarf.

You may like to try stitching the skater's dress in shades of red and adding snow flakes and maybe some green, snowtopped bushes behind her, to create a snowy scene.

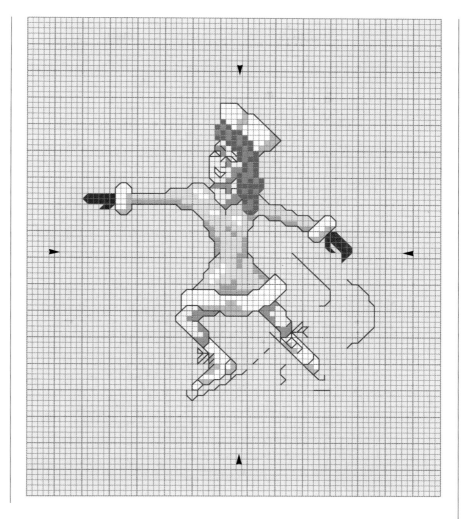

Working the design

Starting at the centre of your fabric, complete all the cross stitch. Using one strand of dark grey cotton, back stitch the figure outline and the detail on the face and boots, including the tracks in the ice.

Finishing

Frame your finished picture as desired. (See Mounting and framing, pages 103–104.)

Materials

Sufficient for one picture

- Stranded embroidery cotton, 1 skein of each colour listed in the key
- Aida fabric, 14HPI, pale green, 8 x 10in (203 x 254mm)
- Flexi-hoop, oval (optional), to fit
- Finished design area: 4 x 4¼in (102 x 114mm)

Key

Colour	Anchor	DMC	Madeira
White	1	Blanc	White
Light blue	159	827	1014
Sea blue	161	826	1012
Nutmeg brown	309	780	2214
Pale beige	366	739	2014
Deep rust brown	371	433	2008
Hessian	373	436	2011
Light grey	398	415	1803
Dark grey	400	317	1714
(Back stitch)			
Dark grey	400	317	1714

Frog and water lily

The aim of this design was to show the pale green background
as a water surface. The frog and lily need to be resting on the surface,
and the reflections in the water solved this problem – if there
were no reflections shown, the effect would be lost.
Faint ripples add to the effect.

Alternatives

Trim the edges of the fabric and sew a neat hem all around, then cover the back of the stitching with a piece of felt, and you will have a bookmark.

You could also make a larger picture by stitching more frogs and water lilies at random, changing the lily colours and adding extra ripples across the water.

Working the design

Cross stitch the frog, water lily and lily pads, using two strands of thread. To stitch the reflection of the frog and the lily, use only one strand of thread. This will give the reflection a paler appearance. Using one strand of cotton, complete all the back stitch as shown on the chart. With one strand of pale yellow thread, cross stitch the small ripples in the water.

Finishing

To finish your picture, you could frame the piece in a decorative flexi-hoop. (See Flexi-hoops, page 105.)

Key

	Colour	Anchor	DMC	Madeira
	Lilac	85	3609	0710
	Dark lilac	87	3607	0708
	Palest green	213	369	1309
	Dark green	246	986	1404
	Lettuce green	254	472	1414
	Bright green	256	906	1411
	Deep moss-green	268	937	1504
	Greengage	280	581	1609
	Light yellow	301	744	0112
	Terracotta	339	920	0312
(Back stitch)				
―――	Dark brown	360	839	1913

Materials

Sufficient for one picture

- Stranded embroidery cotton, 1 skein of each colour listed in the key
- Aida fabric, 14HPI, pale green, 7 x 9in (178 x 229mm)
- Finished design area: 2¼ x 4½in (57 x 114mm)

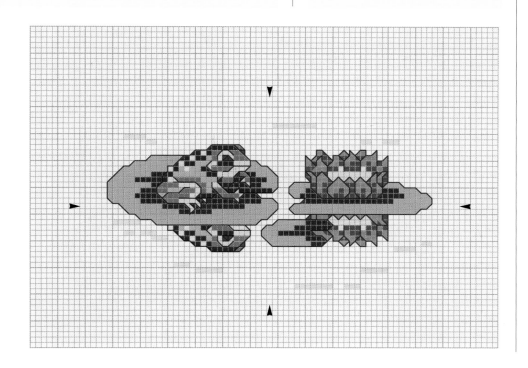

Flowers on trellis

Although ideal for icy themes, pale green fabric can also be used
to add a warm, spring-like touch to a floral picture.
Warm shades are used here, with small white
flowers to soften the edges of the design
and help break up the strong lines of the trellis.

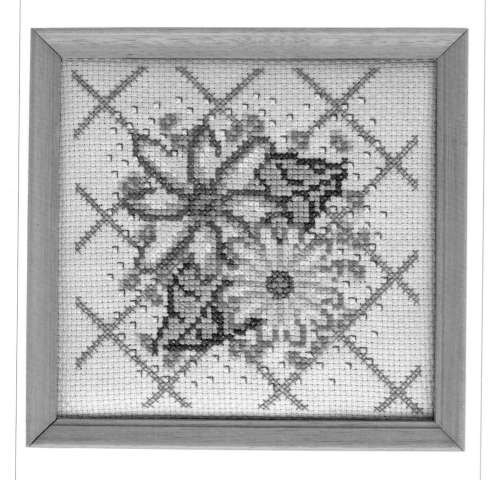

Alternatives

You may like to create a beautiful tablecloth and matching placemats by omitting the trellis work and repeating the floral design as an edging.

You could also make a small drawstring purse for your dressing table. To do this, stitch the flower motif on two pieces of green Aida, 3in (76mm) longer than suggested, and place the design near the bottom of each piece. Join the two together, with right sides facing, along the bottom and two sides. Turn right sides out and hem the top edge. Weave six strands of thread through the top of the purse, about 2in (50mm) from the top edge, beginning at one side seam and leaving several inches of thread at the start and finish. Knot both ends of the thread together and use this tail as the drawstring.

Working the design

Begin at the centre point of both the chart and the fabric, and cross stitch the spray of flowers and central design. Carefully work the trellis pattern using one strand of ginger brown cotton. With one strand of green thread, back stitch along two sides, either the bottom and left side, or the top and right side (see chart and picture) of each individual white cross stitch.

Finishing

For the best effect, mount your finished work in a pale, woodgrain frame. (See Mounting and framing, pages 103–104.)

Materials

Sufficient for one picture

- Stranded embroidery cotton, 1 skein of each colour listed in the key
- Aida Fabric, 14HPI, pale green, 9 x 9in (229 x 229mm)
- Finished design area: 4½x 4½in (114 x 114mm)

Key

	Colour	Anchor	DMC	Madeira
	White	1	Blanc	White
	Pale lilac	90	3609	0710
	Dark mauve	98	553	0712
	Light green	241	368	1310
	Dark green	246	986	1404
	Lettuce green	254	472	1414
	Deep moss green	268	937	1504
	Greengage	280	581	1609
	Yellow	305	743	0113
	Terracotta	339	920	0312
	Dark terracotta	341	918	0314
	Hessian	373	436	2011
	Ginger brown	365	435	2010
(Back stitch)				
	Deep moss green	268	937	1504

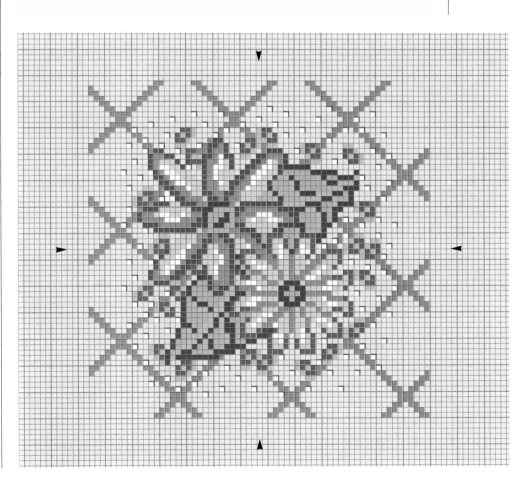

Chapter 10
Framing finished work

A carefully chosen mount or frame can set off
your work and show it at its best.
There is a wide range of frames available, of
different size, shape and colour, so you can pick
and choose to get the effect you want.

Washing stitched fabric
Framing or mounting the design
Finishing without framing

Preparation

To look its best, and for the good of the fabric and threads,
a finished design should be free of dust and grime, and as much care
should be taken in the cleaning, as in the stitching and framing.

Washing the stitched fabric

If a stitched fabric needs washing, this should be done before framing. To wash a completed cross stitch embroidery, gently swish your work in slightly soapy, lukewarm water. If some of

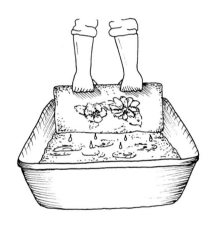

the colours start to bleed, do not remove the fabric from the water: you must keep it under the water until all the bleeding has finished. Once all the bleeding has stopped, remove the fabric from the

water, and rinse it in clean water to wash off any remaining soap. Place the fabric, face down, onto a thick layer of soft towels to stop the stitches from being flattened when pressing. Lay a clean piece of cloth over the fabric and gently iron the fabric until dry.

Mounting and framing

Cross stitch can be finished as a design in its own right,
or given another life and set as a card, a paperweight, a bookmark . . .

Choosing the frame and mount

The method for framing your work will depend on the size of your picture. Wooden frames work well for large pieces; for smaller pictures, the scope for mounting and framing is much greater.

First, choose a frame to fit your design, making sure your fabric will overlap each edge by 1–2in (25–50mm). If you are using glass in your frame, make sure your stitched fabric does not touch the glass, as this will flatten the stitches. You can prevent this by using a picture mount, which is a piece of card with an aperture, or window, cut out of the middle. The mount is placed in between the glass and your stitching. If using a mount, try to match it with one of the colours used in your stitched design for a more harmonious effect. If you are not using glass, you will need to place

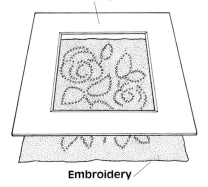

Card mount with aperture

Embroidery

Fig 10.1 A picture mount will keep stitches from becoming flattened

some wadding between the stiff board and your picture to keep the fabric smooth. The 2oz (186.5g) wadding used for quilting is ideal for this purpose.

Mounting the finished project

In order to mount a picture in a wooden frame, you will have to lace the fabric onto mounting board or hardboard. For very small pictures, strong cardboard will suffice.

Cut your board, and wadding

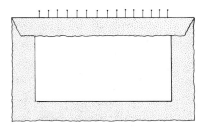

Fig 10.2 To mount the finished project, pin the fabric to the board . . .

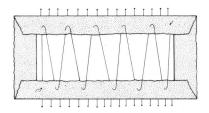

. . . lace the fabric across the back of the board . . .

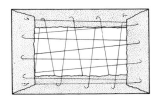

. . . and repeat for the remaining two sides

103

if necessary, so that they fit loosely inside the frame. This is to allow for the extra thickness of your fabric. Centre the board, and wadding, on the back of your fabric, and tack the material to the board, by folding the material over and pinning along one edge. Do the same along the opposite edge, making sure the fabric is flat against the board. Now, using strong thread, preferably thin crochet cotton, lace across the back of the board. Repeat this procedure for the remaining two edges and remove all pins.

Your stitching is now ready to be framed. To do this, place your frame face down on a table, unfastening the clips and removing the backing if the frame is ready backed. Glass is purely optional, so leave the glass in the frame or remove it now, as desired. If you are using a card mount, place this face down in the frame. Place your stitched and laced work face down into the frame and replace or add the backing board. Refasten the frame clips, or if no clips are present, insert veneer pins into the frame to hold the picture in place. Seal the back of the picture with brown gummed tape.

Mounting small designs

For smaller designs, there are alternative frames: they can be mounted in trinkets, on

Fig 10.3 To add faint colour to a card blank, rub a pastel crayon onto scrap paper . . .

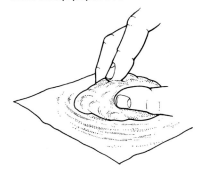

. . . swirl a piece of cotton wool in the pastel dust . . .

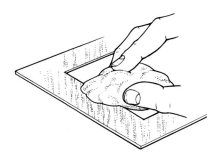

. . . then brush the cotton wool across the card

box lids, in paperweights, and even on spoons. They can also be mounted in special greetings cards or bookmarks. These have a variety of aperture shapes through which to see your stitching.

Before mounting your design in a card or bookmark,

you might like to add some colour to the card blank, as can be seen on the rosebud bookmark on page 76. To do this, rub a coloured pastel crayon onto a piece of scrap paper to create some dust. Take a piece of cotton wool and swirl it in the pastel dust, then brush the cotton wool across the front of your card blank, where you want the specks of colour to be.

To mount a picture in a card or bookmark, proceed as follows:

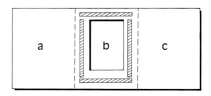

Fig 10.4 To mount a picture in a card or bookmark, stick double-sided tape around the aperture . . .

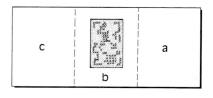

. . . centre the card over the picture . . .

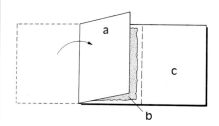

. . . stick double-sided tape around the edge of one side, fold and press down

1 Open the card and place face down on a flat surface.

2 Stick double-sided tape all round the edges of the aperture. (Avoid using glue as this may eventually discolour the fabric).

3 Hold the card face up and place centrally over your stitched piece. Press down firmly so that the fabric sticks to the tape.

4 Turn the card over again, and place strips of double-sided tape around the edges of side *a*.

5 Fold side *a* over onto side *b*, and press down. Your card is now complete and may be left as it is, or placed in a wooden frame.

Flexi-hoops

As suggested before, you may want to frame your design in a flexi-hoop. To do this, separate the inner and outer rings of the hoop, cut a circle of felt the same size as the inner ring, and proceed as follows:

1 Place your finished design over the inner ring and push the outer ring back in place over your fabric.

2 Turn the hoop over so that the design is face down, and cut away the excess fabric (shaded on diagram), leaving about 1½in (38mm) all around the edge.

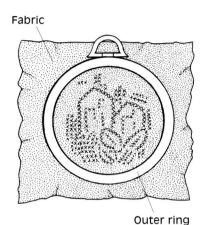

Fabric

Outer ring

Fig 10.5 To frame a design in a flexi-hoop, place design over inner ring and push outer ring over fabric . . .

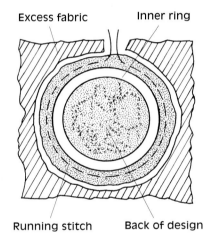

Excess fabric

Inner ring

Running stitch

Back of design

. . . cut away excess fabric, sew a ring of running stitch, pull and tie the loose ends to gather edging . . .

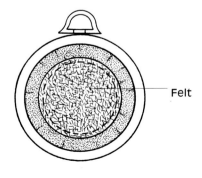

Felt

. . . then cover with felt backing

3 Sew a row of running stitch 1in (25mm) from the hoop, all around, leaving approximately 3in (76mm) of thread loose at the beginning, and again at the end. Carefully pull the two ends of the thread so that the edging gathers up. Tie the two ends together tightly to fasten off.

4 Cover the gathered edging by stitching the felt circle to the back.

Finishing without framing

If you do not wish to frame your finished picture, you could hem the edges of the fabric to prevent them from fraying, and then trim them with decorative lace.

These are just a few framing ideas to help you get the most from your pictures – the choice is yours.

Metric conversion table

Inches to millimetres and centimetres

mm – millimetres   cm – centimetres

inches	mm	cm	inches	cm	inches	cm
⅛	3	0.3	9	22.9	30	76.2
¼	6	0.6	10	25.4	31	78.7
⅜	10	1.0	11	27.9	32	81.3
½	13	1.3	12	30.5	33	83.8
⅝	16	1.6	13	33.0	34	86.4
¾	19	1.9	14	35.6	35	88.9
⅞	22	2.2	15	38.1	36	91.4
1	25	2.5	16	40.6	37	94.0
1¼	32	3.2	17	43.2	38	96.5
1½	38	3.8	18	45.7	39	99.1
1¾	44	4.4	19	48.3	40	101.6
2	51	5.1	20	50.8	41	104.1
2½	64	6.4	21	53.3	42	106.7
3	76	7.6	22	55.9	43	109.2
3½	89	8.9	23	58.4	44	111.8
4	102	10.2	24	61.0	45	114.3
4½	114	11.4	25	63.5	46	116.8
5	127	12.7	26	66.0	47	119.4
6	152	15.2	27	68.6	48	121.9
7	178	17.8	28	71.1	49	124.5
8	203	20.3	29	73.7	50	127.0

About the author

Sheena Rogers' interest in cross stitch began one Christmas with her acquisition of a small cross stitch kit. Having enjoyed drawing and painting for many years, she wanted to try something new. Immediately hooked, she now combines her cross stitch and drawing skills in designing new patterns, and has had a number of her designs published in needlework magazines.

She also designs tapestries, and enjoys experimenting with different materials, such as beads and glitter threads, in her work. Knitting toys and quilting are among her other skills, and her interest in crafts, particularly so with cross stitch and embroidery, extends to their history and development, about which she is an avid reader.

Titles available from GMC Publications

Videos

Dennis White Teaches Woodturning

    Part 1 Turning Between Centres

    Part 2 Turning Bowls

    Part 3 Boxes, Goblets and Screw Threads

    Part 4 Novelties and Projects

    Part 5 Classic Profiles

    Part 6 Twists and Advanced Turning

John Jordan   Bowl Turning

John Jordan   Hollow Turning

Jim Kingshott   Sharpening the Professional Way

Jim Kingshott   Sharpening Turning and Carving Tools

Ray Gonzalez   Carving a Figure: The Female Form

David James   The Traditional Upholstery Workshop Part I: Drop-in and Pinstuffed Seats

David James   The Traditional Upholstery Workshop Part II: Stuffover Upholstery

GMC Publications regularly produces new books and videos on a wide range of woodworking and craft subjects, and an increasing number of specialist magazines, all available on subscription:

Magazines

WOODTURNING   **WOODCARVING**   **BUSINESSMATTERS**

All these publications are available through bookshops and newsagents, or may be ordered by post from the publishers at:
166 High Street, Lewes, East Sussex BN7 1XU
Telephone (01273) 477374, Fax (01273) 478606
Credit card orders are accepted

PLEASE WRITE OR PHONE FOR A FREE CATALOGUE